Cherries in the Summer

"There is no stranger under the cherry tree."
Kobayashi Issa

Written by: Kevin Carroll
Illustrated by: Vivian Nguyen

Balboa Press books may be ordered through booksellers or by contacting:

Balboa Press
A Division of Hay House
1663 Liberty Drive
Bloomington, IN 47403
www.balboapress.com
844-682-1282

Because of the dynamic nature of the Internet, any web addresses or links contained in this book may have changed since publication and may no longer be valid. The views expressed in this work are solely those of the author and do not necessarily reflect the views of the publisher, and the publisher hereby disclaims any responsibility for them.

Interior Image Credit: Vivian Nguyen

ISBN: 978-1-9822-7467-2 (sc)
ISBN: 978-1-9822-7466-5 (e)

Print information available on the last page.

Balboa Press rev. date: 09/23/2021

BALBOA.PRESS
A DIVISION OF HAY HOUSE

This book is dedicated to

...my parents, who have supported me unconditionally, especially during the illustrating of this book.

Vivian

...the administration, faculty, and staff of St. Victor School in San José, California, who provide a nurturing environment of faith and learning for their students.

Kevin

A bowl of
fresh-picked
cherries,

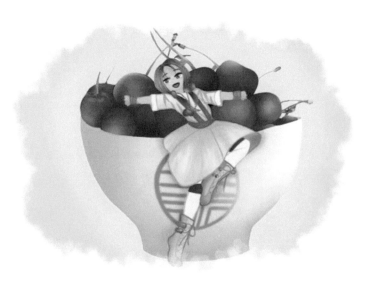

a treasure
to be shared.

Each cherry has
a hidden pit!

You need to
be prepared.

A bowl of
fresh-picked
cherries,

a very
special treat.

They're fairly inexpensive,

and incredible to eat.

Cherry Cobbler,
cherry pie,

cherry
cheesecake, too.

A cherry on
a sundae

made
especially
for you!

Black cherry
ice cream

or
Cherries Jubilee,

this tiny, red,
delicious fruit

is good for
you and me.

Cherries grow on
cherry trees,

mostly in
the summer.

A day without
some fresh-picked
cherries

really is
a bummer.

Kids like
cherry Popsicles

and some like
Cherry Coke.

They certainly
taste better

than a giant
artichoke!

Even in
a bakery,

cherries can
be found,

on yummy
Danish pastries.

You can
pass them
all around!

Cherry-almond
breakfast bars,

and cherry
muffins, too.

Chocolate
cherry brownies

are waiting
there for you.

Cherries can
be added

to your breakfast
or your lunch.

You may want
just a handful,

or you might
prefer a bunch.

Cherries are
delicious,

and very
healthy, too.

Be sure to
have a
good supply,

especially
for you.

Cherries,
cherries
everywhere!

So good
for you
to eat.

Throughout
the warmer
summer months

they're such
a tasty treat.

One secret
about cherries,

which you should
be aware…

they always taste
much better

when we
generously
share!

About the Author and Illustrator

Kevin Carroll was a teacher of middle school and high school students for forty years. He retired in June 2015. In October 2017, he published his first book, *A Moment's Pause for Gratitude*. Unexpectedly, in November 2019, he accepted a long-term substitute teaching position at St. Victor School in San José, California. It was there that he met Vivian Nguyen, who was one of his students. Kevin is now retired, once again, and focusing on writing.

Vivian Nguyen is currently in seventh grade at St. Victor School. She started drawing at the age of seven, but didn't begin working on it as a craft until she was ten years old. Vivian enjoys reading manga and listening to K-Pop music. She occasionally works on scrapbooking, too. Her favorite type of literature is realistic fiction. Vivian is aiming for a career as a planner or business person.

Printed in the United States
by Baker & Taylor Publisher Services